THAI CUISINE 2022

TASTY AND EASY RECIPES FROM THE TRADITION

SEAN SMIT

Table of Contents

Crab Spring Rolls

Break out your wok — it was made for dishes like this! Consider adding another layer of flavor by throwing a half pound deveined, chopped shrimp into the mix.

Yields 15 rolls

∽

Ingredients

1 pound crabmeat, picked over to remove any shells, and shredded

1 tablespoon mayonnaise

¼–½ teaspoon grated lime peel

15 spring roll or egg roll wrappers

2 egg yolks, lightly beaten

Canola oil for deep frying

15 small, tender Boston lettuce leaves

Mint leaves

Parsley leaves

1. In a small bowl, mix the crabmeat with the mayonnaise and lime peel.

2. Place 1 tablespoon of the crabmeat mixture in the center of 1 spring roll wrapper. Fold a pointed end of the wrapper over the crabmeat, then fold the opposite point over the top of the folded point. Brush a bit of the egg yolk over the top of the exposed wrapper, then fold the bottom point over the crabmeat and roll to form a tight packet; set aside. Repeat with the remaining crabmeat and wrappers.

3. Heat the oil to 365 degrees in a skillet or deep fryer. Deep-fry the rolls 3 to 4 at a time for 2 minutes or so, until they are a golden brown; drain on paper towels.

4. To serve, wrap each spring roll in a wrapper with a single piece of lettuce, and a sprinkling of mint and parsley. Serve with your favorite dipping sauce.

Thai Fries

Your local Asian market should carry ingredients like taro root and sticky rice flour (aka glutinous rice flour or sweet rice flour). The latter is also widely available online.

Serves 4-8

Ingredients

2 medium-sized sweet potatoes

4 green plantains

1 pound taro root

1 cup rice flour

1 cup sticky rice flour

Water

1 teaspoon black pepper

1 teaspoon salt

2 tablespoons sugar

3 tablespoons black sesame seeds

1 14-ounce bag shredded sweetened coconut

1. Peel the root vegetables and cut them into flat ⅓-inch-thick strips about 3 inches long and 1 inch wide.

2. Combine the flours in a large mixing bowl and stir in ½ cup of water. Continue adding water ¼ cup at a time until a mixture resembling pancake batter is formed. Stir in remaining ingredients.

3. Fill a medium-sized saucepan a third to a half full with vegetable oil. Heat the oil over high heat until very hot, but not smoking.

4. Add some of the vegetables to the batter, coating them well. Using a slotted spoon or Asian strainer, place the vegetables in the hot oil. (Be careful here: The oil may spatter.) Fry the vegetables, turning them occasionally, until golden brown. Transfer the fried vegetables to a stack of paper towels to drain, then serve immediately.

Fried Wontons

When lighter spring rolls won't cut it, opt for these satisfying wontons! Get creative with the filling; substitute chicken for pork or add shredded cabbage for a vegetarian version.

Yields approximately 25 wontons

Ingredients

1 clove garlic, minced

2 tablespoons cilantro, minced

1 tablespoon soy sauce

½ cup white mushrooms, chopped

Pinch white pepper

½ pound ground pork

25 wonton skins

Vegetable oil for frying

1. In a medium-sized mixing bowl, thoroughly combine the garlic, cilantro, soy sauce, mushrooms, white pepper, and ground pork.

2. To make the wontons, place approximately ½ teaspoon of the filling in the middle of a wonton skin. Fold the wonton from corner to corner, forming a triangle. Press the edges together to seal closed. Repeat with the remaining skins and filling.

3. Add about 2 to 3 inches of vegetable oil to a deep fryer or wok. Heat the oil on medium until it reaches about 350 degrees. Carefully add the wontons, two or three at a time. Fry until they are golden brown, turning them constantly. Transfer the cooked wontons to drain on paper towels as they are done.

4. Serve the wontons with either sweet-and-sour sauce or the sauce of your choice.

Fried Tofu with Dipping Sauces

Tofu comes in different textures: silken, firm, and extra firm. For best — and healthiest — results, go with extra firm, non-GMO tofu and drain and press between paper towels or clean dishtowels before cubing and plunging into prepped oil.

❧

Serves 2-4

Ingredients

1 package of tofu, cut into bite-sized cubes

Vegetable oil for frying

Dipping sauces of your choice

1. Add about 2 to 3 inches of vegetable oil to a deep fryer or wok. Heat the oil on medium until it reaches about 350 degrees. Carefully add some of the tofu pieces, making sure not to overcrowd them; fry until golden brown, turning constantly. Transfer the fried tofu to paper towels to drain as each batch is cooked.

2. Serve the tofu with a choice of dipping sauces, such
    as sweet-and-sour sauce, peanut sauce, or mint
    sauce.

Tom Yum

A staple in Thai cooking, fresh, fragrant lemongrass is sold in bunches of three to five that are about one foot long. You can also find ready-to-use varieties in the freezer section of an Asian market.

Serves 4-6

Ingredients

4–5 cups water

3 shallots, finely chopped

2 stalks lemongrass, bruised and cut into 1-inch-long segments

2 tablespoons fish sauce

2 tablespoons fresh ginger, minced

20 medium-sized shrimp, shelled but with tails left on

1 can straw mushrooms, drained

2–3 teaspoons sliced kaffir lime leaves or lime zest

3 tablespoons lime juice

2–3 Thai chili peppers, seeded and minced

1. Pour the water into a medium-sized soup pot. Add the shallots, lemongrass, fish sauce, and ginger. Bring to a boil, reduce heat, and simmer for 3 minutes.

2. Add the shrimp and mushrooms, and cook until the shrimp turn pink. Stir in the lime zest, lime juice, and chili peppers.

3. Cover and remove from the heat. Let the soup steep for 5 to 10 minutes before serving.

Chicken-Lemon Soup

A mere 40 minutes of prep and cook time allows you to pucker up and enjoy this slightly sweet, slightly pungent soup, which is packed full of classic Thai ingredients.

Serves 4-6

Ingredients

½ cup lemon slices, including peel

3 tablespoons fish sauce

1½ teaspoons fresh hot chili pepper, seeded and chopped

2 green onions, thinly sliced

1½ teaspoons sugar

1½ cups coconut milk

2 cups chicken broth

3 teaspoons lemongrass, peeled and chopped

1 cup straw mushrooms

1 tablespoon fresh ginger, minced

1 whole boneless, skinless chicken breast, poached and shredded

1. Combine the lemon slices, fish sauce, chili pepper, green onion, and sugar in a small glass bowl; set aside.

2. Combine the coconut milk, chicken broth, lemongrass, mushrooms, and ginger in a saucepan. Bring to a boil, reduce heat, and simmer for 20 to 25 minutes. Add the chicken and lemon mixture; heat through.

3. To serve, ladle into warmed bowls.

Thai-Spiced Beef Soup with Noodles

If you stock your pantry with such Thai spices and staples as fish sauce, chili sauce, ginger, and rice noodles, you'll be able to whip up an elegant soup like this whenever you have leftover beef in your fridge.

Serves 4-6

Ingredients

8 cups beef broth

1 whole star anise, crushed

1 (2-inch) cinnamon stick

2 (¼-inch) pieces peeled gingerroot

8 ounces rice noodles, soaked in hot water for 10 minutes, strained and rinsed in cold water

1 stalk lemongrass, tough outer leaves removed, inner core crushed and minced

¾ cup leftover beef roast, chopped or shredded

¼ cup fish sauce

1 tablespoon prepared chili-garlic sauce

2½ tablespoons lime juice

3–4 teaspoons (or to taste) salt

Freshly ground black pepper to taste

1. In a medium-sized saucepan, simmer the beef broth, star anise, cinnamon stick, and ginger over low heat for 30 to 40 minutes.

2. Strain the stock and return to the saucepan.

3. Add the noodles, lemongrass, shredded beef, fish sauce, chili sauce, and garlic. Bring the soup to a boil over medium heat. Reduce heat and simmer for 5 minutes. Stir in the lime juice, salt, and pepper.

Chilled Mango Soup

To cut the sweetness even more and give this savory soup some kick, leave out the sugar and instead add a dash of cayenne and red pepper flakes.

Serves 2-4

Ingredients

2 large mangoes, peeled, pitted, and chopped

1½ cups chicken or vegetable broth, chilled

1 cup plain yogurt

1 teaspoon sugar (optional)

1 tablespoon dry sherry

Salt and white pepper to taste

1. Place all of the ingredients in a blender or food processor and process until smooth. Adjust seasonings.

2. This soup may be served immediately or refrigerated until needed. If you do refrigerate the soup, let it sit

at room temperature for 10 minutes or so before serving to take some of the chill off.

Fiery Beef Salad

Serve as a hearty entrée salad or reduce the serving size and present as a piquant first course. Either way, you'll want to make extra dressing to keep on hand!

Serves 2-4

Ingredients

For the dressing:

¼ cup basil leaves

2 tablespoons serrano chilies, chopped

2 cloves garlic

2 tablespoons brown sugar

2 tablespoons fish sauce

¼ teaspoon black pepper

¼ cup lemon juice

For the salad:

1 pound beef steak

Salt and pepper to taste

1 stalk lemongrass, outer leaves removed and discarded, inner stalk finely sliced

1 small red onion, finely sliced

1 small cucumber, finely sliced

1 tomato, finely sliced

½ cup mint leaves

Bibb or romaine lettuce leaves

1. Combine all of the dressing ingredients in a blender and process until well incorporated; set aside.

2. Season the steak with salt and pepper. Over a hot fire, grill to medium-rare (or to your liking). Transfer the steak to a platter, cover with foil, and let rest for 5 to 10 minutes before carving.

3. Slice the beef across the grain into thin slices.

4. Place the beef slices, any juices from the platter, and the remaining salad ingredients, except the lettuce, in a large mixing bowl. Add the dressing and toss to coat.

5. To serve, place lettuce leaves on individual plates and mound the beef mixture on top of the lettuce.

Spicy Shrimp Salad

The heat of the chili sauce plays off the fresh flavors of lime and mint in this memorable salad. Best of all, it comes together in a pinch.

Serves 2-4

Ingredients

For the dressing:

3 tablespoons sugar

4 tablespoons fish sauce

⅓ cup lime juice

2 tablespoons prepared chili sauce

For the salad:

¾ pound cooked shrimp

¼ cup mint, chopped

1 small red onion, thinly sliced

2 green onions, trimmed and thinly sliced

2 cucumbers, peeled and thinly sliced

Bibb lettuce leaves

1. In a small bowl, combine all the dressing ingredients. Stir until the sugar dissolves completely.

2. In a large bowl, combine all of the salad ingredients except the lettuce. Pour the dressing over and toss to coat.

3. To serve, place the lettuce leaves on individual plates. Mound a portion of the shrimp salad on top of the leaves. Serve immediately.

Sweet-and-Sour Cucumber Salad

This lip-smacking recipe is in effect a quick pickling; to intensify the flavors, leave in the fridge for even longer!

Serves 2-4

Ingredients

5 tablespoons sugar

1 teaspoon salt

1 cup boiling water

½ cup rice or white vinegar

2 medium cucumbers, seeded and sliced

1 small red onion, sliced

2 Thai chilies, seeded and minced

1. In a small bowl, combine the sugar, salt, and boiling water. Stir to thoroughly dissolve sugar and salt. Add the vinegar and allow the vinaigrette to cool to room temperature.

2. Place the cucumbers, onion slices, and the chili peppers in a medium-sized bowl. Pour the dressing over the vegetables. Cover and let marinate in the refrigerator at least until cold, preferably overnight.

Zesty Melon Salad

A quintessential summer dish, pair this with grilled meat and a chilled savory noodle dish for an impressive Thai dinner meant to be enjoyed outdoors.

Serves 4-6

Ingredients

6 cups assorted melon cubes

2 cucumbers, peeled, halved, seeded, and sliced

6–8 tablespoons lime juice

Zest of 1 lime

¼ cup honey

1 serrano chili, seeded and minced (for a hotter salad, leave the seeds in)

¼ teaspoon salt

1. In a large mixing bowl, combine the melon and the cucumber.

2. Mix the remaining ingredients together in a small
   bowl. Pour over the fruit and toss well to coat.

3. Serve immediately, or if you like a zestier flavor, let
   the salad sit for up to 2 hours to allow the chili flavor
   to develop.

Hot and Sour Beef

Dark sweet soy sauce, which contains molasses, gives this dish a distinctly different flavor, so resist the urge to substitute with traditional soy, which is not as rich and is much saltier.

Serves 1-2

Ingredients

1 tablespoon lime juice

1 tablespoon fish sauce

1 tablespoon dark, sweet soy sauce

3 tablespoons onion, chopped

1 teaspoon honey

1 teaspoon dried chili powder

1 green onion, trimmed and thinly sliced

1 teaspoon cilantro, chopped

1½ pound sirloin steak

Salt and pepper to taste

1. Make the sauce by thoroughly combining the first eight ingredients; set aside.

2. Season the steak with salt and pepper, then grill or broil it to your preferred doneness. Remove the steak from the grill, cover with foil, and let rest for 5 to 10 minutes.

3. Thinly slice the steak, cutting across the grain.

4. Arrange the pieces on a serving platter or on 1 or 2 dinner plates. Spoon the sauce over the top. Serve with rice and a side vegetable.

Stir-Fried Beef with Mint

Set your rice out in the slow cooker in the morning and you can have dinner on the table in a matter of minutes with this quick, easy, and crowd-pleasing stir-fry.

Serves 4-6

Ingredients

7–14 (to taste) serrano chilies, seeded and coarsely chopped

¼ cup garlic, chopped

¼ cup yellow or white onion, chopped

¼ cup vegetable oil

1 pound flank steak, sliced across the grain into thin strips

3 tablespoons fish sauce

1 tablespoon sugar

½–¾ cup water

½ cup mint leaves, chopped

1. Using a mortar and pestle or a food processor, grind together the chilies, garlic, and onion.

2. Heat the oil over medium-high heat in a wok or large skillet. Add the ground chili mixture to the oil and stir-fry for 1 to 2 minutes.

3. Add the beef and stir-fry until it just begins to brown.

4. Add the remaining ingredients, adjusting the amount of water depending on how thick you want the sauce.

5. Serve with plenty of jasmine rice.

Pork with Garlic and Black Pepper

If you don't own one, invest in a mortar and pestle — a tool that makes mashing the garlic in this recipe an easy task and allows you to release intense flavors from herbs and spices.

Serves 2

Ingredients

10–20 garlic cloves, mashed

2–2½ teaspoons black peppercorns, coarsely ground

4 tablespoons vegetable oil

1 pork tenderloin, trimmed of all fat and cut into medallions about ¼-inch thick

¼ cup sweet black soy sauce

2 tablespoons brown sugar

2 tablespoons fish sauce

1. Place the garlic and the black pepper in a small food processor and process briefly to form a coarse paste; set aside.

2. Heat the oil in a wok or large skillet over medium-high heat. When the oil is hot, add the garlic-pepper paste and stir-fry until the garlic turns gold.

3. Raise the heat to high and add the pork medallions; stir-fry for 30 seconds.

4. Add the soy sauce and brown sugar, stirring until the sugar is dissolved.

5. Add the fish sauce and continue to cook until the pork is cooked through, about another 1 to 2 minutes.

Cinnamon Beef

Cinnamon has been shown to have positive effects on cholesterol and type-2 diabetes. It also has anti-inflammatory properties, so add spice to your beef and gain health benefits in the process!

Serves 4

Ingredients

1½ quarts water

2 tablespoons sugar

2 whole star anise

5 tablespoons soy sauce

1 clove garlic, smashed

2 tablespoons sweet soy sauce

1 (2-inch) piece of cinnamon stick

5 sprigs cilantro

1 celery stalk, sliced

1 pound beef sirloin, trimmed of all fat and cut into 1-inch cubes

1 bay leaf

1. Place the water in a large soup pot and bring to a boil. Reduce heat to low and add the remaining ingredients.

2. Simmer, adding more water if necessary, for at least 2 hours or until the beef is completely tender. If possible, let the stewed beef sit in the refrigerator overnight.

3. To serve, place noodles or rice in the bottom of 4 soup bowls. Add pieces of beef and then ladle broth over. Sprinkle with chopped cilantro or sliced green onions if you like. Pass a vinegar-chili sauce of your choice as a dip for the beef.

Ginger Chicken

Fresh grated ginger is always the ideal choice for the brightest flavor in Thai cooking, but you can extend the life of your roots indefinitely by peeling, chopping, and submerging them in vodka.

Serves 2

Ingredients

2 tablespoons fish sauce

2 tablespoons dark soy sauce

2 tablespoons oyster sauce

3 tablespoons vegetable oil

1 tablespoon garlic, choppped

1 whole boneless, skinless chicken breast, cut into bite-sized pieces

1 cup sliced domestic mushrooms

3 tablespoons grated ginger

Pinch of sugar

3 tablespoons onion, chopped

2–3 habanero or bird's eye chilis

Jasmine rice, cooked according to package directions

3 green onions, trimmed and cut into 1-inch pieces

Cilantro to taste

1. In a small bowl combine the fish, soy, and oyster sauces; set aside.

2. Heat the oil in a large wok until very hot. Add the garlic and chicken, and stir-fry just until the chicken begins to change color.

3. Add the reserved sauce and cook until it begins to simmer, stirring constantly.

4. Add the mushrooms, ginger, sugar, onion, and chilies; simmer until the chicken is cooked through, about 8 minutes.

5. To serve, ladle the chicken over jasmine rice and top with green onion and cilantro.

Basil Chicken

For a bolder flavored dish, use Thai basil (which can be identified by its purple stem) instead of sweet basil. You'll detect flavors and aromas of licorice, cinnamon, and mint in this variety.

Serves 4

Ingredients

2 tablespoons fish sauce

1½ tablespoons soy sauce

1 tablespoon water

1½ teaspoons sugar

2 whole boneless, skinless chicken breasts, cut into 1-inch cubes

2 tablespoons vegetable oil

1 large onion, cut into thin slices

3 Thai chilies, seeded and thinly sliced

3 cloves garlic, minced

1½ cups chopped basil leaves, divided

1. In a medium-sized bowl, combine the fish sauce, the soy sauce, water, and sugar. Add the chicken cubes and stir to coat. Let marinate for 10 minutes.

2. In a large skillet or wok, heat oil over medium-high heat. Add the onion and stir-fry for 2 to 3 minutes. Add the chilies and garlic and continue to cook for an additional 30 seconds.

3. Using a slotted spoon, remove the chicken from the marinade and add it to the skillet (reserve the marinade.) Stir-fry until almost cooked through, about 3 minutes.

4. Add the reserved marinade and cook for an additional 30 seconds. Remove the skillet from the heat and stir in 1 cup of the basil.

5. Garnish with the remaining basil, and serve with rice.

Chicken with Black Pepper and Garlic

Cooking this recipe for your family is a great way to gently introduce them to Thai flavors. Serve alongside jasmine rice and some small chunks of fresh mango to really win them over!

Serves 4-6

Ingredients

1 tablespoon whole black peppercorns

5 cloves garlic, cut in half

2 pounds boneless, skinless chicken breasts, cut into strips

⅓ cup fish sauce

3 tablespoons vegetable oil

1 teaspoon sugar

1. Using either a mortar and pestle or a food processor, combine the black peppercorns with the garlic.

2. Place the chicken strips in a large mixing bowl. Add the garlic-pepper mixture and the fish sauce, and stir to combine.

3. Cover the bowl, place in the refrigerator, and let marinate for 20 to 30 minutes.

4. Heat the vegetable oil over medium heat in a wok or skillet. When it is hot, add the chicken mixture and stir-fry until cooked through, about 3 to 5 minutes.

5. Stir in the sugar. Add additional sugar or fish sauce to taste.

Coconut-Chili Chicken

Forget Thai takeout! When you create this from scratch in your own kitchen it takes on a whole new dimension. For a taste of the tropics, this mix of ingredients can't be beat.

Serves 2-3

Ingredients

2–4 serrano chilies, stems and seeds removed

1 stalk lemongrass, inner portion roughly chopped

2 (2-inch-long, ½-inch wide) strips of lime peel

2 tablespoons vegetable oil

½ cup coconut milk

1 whole boneless, skinless chicken breast, cut into thin strips

2–4 tablespoons fish sauce

10–15 basil leaves

1. Place the chilies, lemongrass, and lime peel into a food processor and process until ground.

2. Heat the oil over medium-high heat in a wok or large skillet. Add the chili mixture and sauté for 1 to 2 minutes.

3. Stir in the coconut milk and cook for 2 minutes.

4. Add the chicken and cook until the chicken is cooked through, about 5 minutes.

5. Reduce heat to low and add the fish sauce and basil leaves to taste.

6. Serve with plenty of jasmine rice.

Lime-Ginger Fillets

This dinner packs lots of nutrition and flavor without being a burden to prepare. For a light-flaky fillet, be sure to be vigilant about watching the broiler so you don't overcook.

Serves 2-4

Ingredients

4 tablespoons unsalted butter, at room temperature

2 teaspoons lime zest

½ teaspoon ground ginger

½ teaspoon salt

4 fish fillets, such as whitefish, perch, or pike

Salt and freshly ground black pepper

1. Preheat the broiler.

2. In a small bowl, thoroughly combine the butter, lime zest, ginger, and ½ teaspoon salt.

3. Lightly season the fillets with salt and pepper and place on a baking sheet.

4. Broil for 4 minutes. Brush each fillet with some of the
    lime-ginger butter and continue to broil for 1 minute
    or until the fish is done to your liking.

Quick Asian-Grilled Fish

If you're concerned about sustainability, you may want to consider the source of your fish. According to The Environmental Defense Fund, mackerel is the best choice, followed by black sea bass; Chilean sea bass is on the "eco-worst" list.

❧

Serves 4-6

Ingredients

1 whole fish, such as sea bass or mackerel, cleaned

4 tablespoons cilantro, chopped

3 tablespoons chopped garlic, divided

1 teaspoon freshly ground black pepper

3 tablespoons lime juice

1 tablespoon jalapeño chili peppers, sliced

2 teaspoons brown sugar

1. Quickly rinse the fish under cold water. Pat dry with paper towels. Set the fish on a large sheet of aluminum foil.

2. Place the cilantro, 2 tablespoons of the garlic, and the black pepper in a food processor and process to form a thick paste.

3. Rub the paste all over the fish, both inside and out. Tightly wrap the fish in the foil.

4. To make the sauce, place the remaining garlic, the lime juice, jalapeños, and brown sugar in a food processor and pulse until combined.

5. Place the fish on a prepared grill and cook for 5 to 6 minutes per side or until the flesh is opaque when pierced with the tip of a knife.

6. Serve the fish with the sauce.

Seafood Stir-Fry

Nothing beats fresh fish, but it's cost effective to stock up when your favorites are on sale, freeze them, and break them out when you crave this flavorful stir-fry.

Serves 2-4

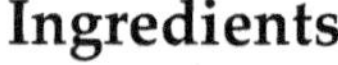

Ingredients

3 tablespoons vegetable oil

3 teaspoons garlic, chopped

2 shallots, chopped

1 stalk lemongrass, bruised

¼ cup basil, chopped

1 can bamboo shoots, rinsed and drained

3 tablespoons fish sauce

Pinch of brown sugar

1 pound fresh shrimp, scallops, or other seafood, cleaned

Rice, cooked according to package directions

1. Heat the oil in a skillet or wok over high heat. Add the garlic, shallots, lemongrass, and basil, and sauté for 1 to 2 minutes.

2. Reduce heat, add the remaining ingredients, and stir-fry until the seafood is done to your liking, approximately 5 minutes.

3. Serve over rice.

Basil Scallops

Kaffir lime leaves impart a unique floral note to any Thai dish. If you can't find them, you can use combo of lime zest and julienned bay leaves for a close substitution.

Serves 2-4

Ingredients

2 tablespoons vegetable oil

3 cloves garlic, chopped

3 kaffir lime leaves, julienned

½ pound bay scallops, cleaned

1 (14-ounce) can straw mushrooms, drained

¼ cup bamboo shoots, shredded

3 tablespoons oyster sauce

15–20 fresh basil leaves

1. In a wok or skillet, heat the oil on high. Add the garlic and lime leaves, and stir-fry until fragrant, about 15 seconds.

2. Add the scallops, mushrooms, bamboo shoots, and oyster sauce; continue to stir-fry for approximately 4 to 5 minutes or until the scallops are done to your liking.

3. Mix in the basil leaves and serve immediately.

Vegetarian Stir-Fry

Use these veggies or others, depending on what you have on hand, but don't wing the step that involves making the sauce — it's what makes this so mouthwateringly delicious.

Serves 4-6 as a main course

Ingredients

1–2 tablespoons vegetable oil

2 cups bite-sized tofu pieces

2 tablespoons garlic, minced

2 tablespoons grated ginger

4 tablespoons Thai chilies, seeded and sliced

4 tablespoons soy sauce

2 tablespoons dark, sweet soy sauce

1 small onion, sliced

¼ cup snow peas

¼ cup celery, thinly sliced

¼ cup water chestnuts

¼ cup bite-sized pieces bell pepper

¼ cup mushrooms, sliced

¼ cup cauliflower florets

¼ cup broccoli florets

¼ cup asparagus tips

1 tablespoon cornstarch, dissolved in a little water

¼ cup bean sprouts

Rice, cooked according to package directions

1. Heat 1 tablespoon of oil in a large skillet or wok over medium-high heat. Add the tofu and sauté until golden brown. Transfer the tofu to paper towels to drain.

2. Add additional oil to the skillet if necessary, and stir-fry the garlic, ginger, and chilies to release their fragrance, about 2 to 3 minutes. Stir in the soy sauces and increase the heat to high.

3. Add the reserved tofu and all the vegetables except the bean sprouts; stir-fry for 1 minute.

4. Add the cornstarch mixture and stir-fry for another minute or until the vegetables are just cooked through and the sauce has thickened slightly.

5. Add the bean sprouts, stirring briefly to warm them.

6. Serve over rice.

Roasted Cauliflower

It doesn't get much easier than this! The marinade breathes life into earthy cauliflower and encourages you to eat more of this nutritious and underrated cruciferous vegetable.

Serves 6-8

Ingredients

1 head cauliflower, broken into florets (cut the florets in half if large)

½ cup marinade or sauce of your choice

1. Place the cauliflower florets in a large zipper storage bag and pour marinade over them; let rest in the refrigerator for 4 to 6 hours.

2. Preheat the oven to 500 degrees.

3. Place the cauliflower florets in a roasting pan. Roast for approximately 15 minutes or until tender, turning after 7 to 8 minutes.

Thai-Style Fried Okra

Tapioca flour is starchy, slightly sweet, grain-free white flour made from cassava root. Commonly used as a thickener, it is necessary here to create a light batter for this unique fried snack.

Yields approximately 20 pieces

Ingredients

⅓ cup all-purpose flour

½ cup tapioca flour

1 teaspoon baking powder

½ cup water

1 pound small okra, trimmed

1 cup vegetable oil

½ cup chili dipping sauce of your choice

1. In a medium-sized mixing bowl, combine the flours, the baking soda, and water to form a batter. Add the okra pieces.

2. Heat the vegetable oil in a frying pan or wok over high heat. (It should be hot enough that a test piece of batter puffs up immediately.)

3. Add the battered okra, a few at a time, and fry until golden.

4. Using a slotted spoon, remove the okra to paper towels to drain.

5. Serve hot with your favorite chili dipping sauce.

Stir-Fried Snap Peas and Bean Sprouts

Savor the crunchy fresh flavor of this unadulterated dish, which pairs nicely with a jasmine brown rice and crushed peanuts for a vegetarian entrée.

Serves 4-6

Ingredients

2 tablespoons vegetable oil

1 small onion, thinly sliced

1 (1-inch) piece ginger, peeled and minced

Pinch of white pepper

1 tablespoon soy sauce

½ pound sugar snap peas, trimmed

1 pound bean sprouts, rinsed thoroughly and trimmed if necessary

Salt and sugar to taste

1. Heat the vegetable oil over medium-high heat in a large skillet.

2. Add the onion and the ginger and sauté for 1 minute.

3. Stir in the white pepper and the soy sauce.

4. Add the sugar snap peas and cook, stirring constantly, for 1 minute.

5. Add the bean sprouts and cook for 1 more minute while stirring constantly.

6. Add up to ½ teaspoon of salt and a large pinch of sugar to adjust the balance of the sauce. Serve immediately.

Pad Thai

In Thailand, this ubiquitous dish is eaten as a light meal and is a favorite at night markets. A potentially unfamiliar ingredient here is Tamarind concentrate, which comes from the pod of a tree native to Africa, but is now mostly cultivated in India.

Serves 2-4

Ingredients

8 ounces rice noodles

2 tablespoons vegetable oil

5–6 cloves garlic, finely chopped

2 tablespoons shallots, chopped

½ cup cooked salad shrimp

¼ cup fish sauce

¼ cup brown sugar

6–8 teaspoons tamarind concentrate

¼ cup chives, chopped

½ cup roasted peanuts, chopped

1 medium egg, beaten

1 cup bean sprouts

Garnish:

1 tablespoon lime juice

1 tablespoon tamarind concentrate

1 tablespoon fish sauce

½ cup bean sprouts

½ cup chives, chopped

½ cup roasted peanuts, coarsely ground

1 lime cut into wedges

1. Soak the noodles in water at room temperature for 30 minutes or until soft. Drain and set aside.

2. Heat the vegetable oil in a wok or skillet over medium-high heat. Add the garlic and shallots, and briefly stir-fry until they begin to change color.

3. Add the reserved noodles and all the remaining ingredients except the egg and the bean sprouts, and stir-fry until hot.

4. While constantly stirring, slowly drizzle in the beaten
    egg.

5. Add the bean sprouts and cook for no more than
    another 30 seconds.

6. In a small bowl mix together all of the garnish
    ingredients except the lime wedges.

7. To serve, arrange the Pad Thai on a serving platter.
    Top with the garnish and surround with lime
    wedges.

Pan-Fried Noodles

This crunchy dish makes a perfect bed for marinated meat or steamed vegetables. Adjust the chili-garlic paste according to how much flavor you'd like to pack in!

Serves 6-8

Ingredients

¾ pound fresh lo mein noodles or angel hair pasta

¼ cup minced chives

2 tablespoons (or to taste) prepared chili-garlic paste

3 tablespoons vegetable oil, divided

Salt to taste

1. Boil the noodles in a large pot for no more than 2 to 3 minutes. Drain, rinse under cold water, and drain again.

2. Add the chives, chili paste, 1 tablespoon of the oil, and salt to the noodles; toss to coat, and adjust seasonings.

3. In a heavy-bottomed 10-inch skillet, heat the
   remaining oil over medium-high heat. When it is hot,
   add the noodle mixture, spreading evenly. Press the
   noodles into the pan with the back of a spatula. Cook
   for approximately 2 minutes. Reduce heat and
   continue to cook until the noodles are nicely
   browned. Flip the noodles over in 1 piece. Continue
   cooking until browned, adding additional oil if
   necessary.

4. To serve, cut the noodles into wedges.

Vegetarian Sesame Noodles

While you can use regular egg noodles for this, you'll get a distinctly different dish by seeking out Asian egg noodles, which are not wide and flat but thin and a bit more dense.

Serves 2-4

Ingredients

2 tablespoons vegetable oil

2 cloves garlic, minced

2 cups broccoli, cut into bite-sized pieces

1 red bell pepper, seeded and cut into strips

2 tablespoons water

8 ounces egg noodles

4 ounces tofu, cut into bite-sized cubes

1 tablespoon sesame oil

2–3 tablespoons soy sauce

2–3 tablespoons prepared chili sauce

3 tablespoons sesame seeds

1. Heat the oil in a large sauté pan or wok over medium heat. Add the garlic and sauté until golden, approximately 2 minutes.

2. Add the broccoli and red bell pepper, and stir-fry for 2 to 3 minutes. Add the water, cover, and let the vegetables steam until tender, approximately 5 minutes.

3. Bring a large pot of water to boil. Add the noodles and cook until al dente; drain.

4. While the noodles are cooking, add the remaining ingredients to the broccoli mixture. Remove from heat, add the noodles, and toss to combine.

Flowered Lime Noodles

The hybrid of Thai and Italian flavors sing in this unique dish. Edible flowers such as nasturtiums and Johnny Jump-Ups are easy to grow and are often available at your local farm stand.

Serves 4

Ingredients

8 ounces angel hair pasta

1 tablespoon salted butter

2–3 tablespoons lime juice

4 ounces grated Parmesan cheese

Rose petals or other organic edible flowers

Lime slices

Black pepper

1. Bring a large pot of water to a boil over high heat. Add pasta and cook according to package instructions; drain.

2. Toss the pasta with butter, lime juice, and parmesan.

3. To serve, top with rose or flower petals and lime
    slices. Pass black pepper at the table.

Broccoli Noodles with Garlic and Soy

For a heartier meal, add more of your favorite green veggies and a thinly sliced chicken breast to your sauté. (Just remember to increase the sauce ingredients accordingly!)

Serves 2-4

Ingredients

1 pound broccoli, trimmed into bite-sized florets

16 ounces rice noodles

1–2 tablespoons vegetable oil

2 cloves garlic, minced

2 tablespoons soy sauce

1 tablespoon sweet soy sauce

1 tablespoon sugar

Hot sauce

Fish sauce

Lime wedges

1. Bring a pot of water to boil over high heat. Drop in the broccoli and blanch until tender-crisp or to your liking. Drain and set aside.

2. Soak the rice noodles in hot water until soft, about 10 minutes.

3. In a large sauté pan, heat the vegetable oil on medium. Add the garlic and stir-fry until golden. Add the soy sauces and the sugar, stirring until the sugar has completely dissolved.

4. Add the reserved noodles, tossing until well coated with the sauce. Add the broccoli and toss to coat.

5. Serve immediately with hot sauce, fish sauce, and lime wedges on the side.

Basic Sticky Rice

In Thailand, this staple food is steamed in large funnels; here you'll use a steamer basket. Found at any Asian market, it's also called "sweet rice," "mochi rice," or "sticky rice."

Serves 2-4

❧

Ingredients

1 cup glutinous rice

Water

1. Place the rice in a bowl, completely cover it with water, and let soak overnight. Drain before using.

2. Line a steamer basket or colander with moistened cheesecloth. (This prevents the grains of rice from falling through the holes in the colander.)

3. Spread the rice over the cheesecloth as evenly as you can.

4. Bring a pan of water with a cover to a rolling boil. Place the basket over the boiling water, making sure

that the bottom of it does not touch the water. Cover

tightly and let steam for 25 minutes.

Far East Fried Rice

Opt for vegetarian fish sauce and drop the egg to create a vegan version. Or, make it meaty by adding shredded leftover chicken or beef. The variations are endless!

Serves 4-6

Ingredients

2 tablespoons fish sauce

1½ tablespoons rice vinegar

2 tablespoons sugar

2½ tablespoons vegetable oil

2 eggs, beaten

1 bunch green onions, trimmed and thinly sliced

2 tablespoons garlic, minced

1 teaspoon dried red chili pepper flakes

2 large carrots, peeled and coarsely shredded

2 cups bean sprouts, trimmed if necessary

5 cups day-old long-grain white rice, clumps broken up

¼ cup mint or cilantro leaves, chopped

¼ cup roasted peanuts, chopped

1. Combine the fish sauce, rice vinegar, and sugar in a small bowl; set aside.

2. In a wok or large skillet, heat the oil over medium-high heat. Add the eggs and stir-fry until scrambled.

3. Add the green onions, garlic, and pepper flakes and continue to stir-fry for 15 seconds or until fragrant.

4. Add the carrots and bean sprouts; stir-fry until the carrots begin to soften, about 2 minutes.

5. Add the rice and cook for 2 to 3 minutes or until heated through.

6. Stir in the fish sauce mixture and add the fried rice, tossing until evenly coated.

7. To serve, garnish the rice with chopped mint, or cilantro, and chopped peanuts.

Ginger Rice

The sweet, spicy flavor of fresh gingerroot lingers and grows more complex as it's allowed to cook into a dish. It'll wake up your tastebuds and help boost your energy!

Serves 4-6

Ingredients

2 tablespoons vegetable oil

1 (½-inch) piece of gingerroot, peeled and thinly sliced

1 stalk lemongrass, sliced into rings (tender inner portion only)

2–3 green onions, sliced into rings

1 red chili pepper, seeded and minced

1½ cups long-grained rice

Pinch of brown sugar

Pinch of salt

Juice of ½ lime

2¾ cups water

1. In a medium-sized pot, heat the oil over medium heat. Add the gingerroot, lemongrass, green onions, and chili pepper; sauté for 2 to 3 minutes.

2. Add the rice, brown sugar, salt, and lime juice, and continue to sauté for an additional 2 minutes. Add the water to the pot and bring to a boil.

3. Reduce the heat, cover with a tight-fitting lid, and simmer for 15 to 20 minutes, until the liquid is absorbed.

Tropical Coconut Rice

Rice comprises the base of many Thai desserts, and this is no different. Coconut and fruit such as pineapple, mango, banana, or guava

combine to make it creamy and sweet.

Serves 6-8

Ingredients

2 cups short-grained rice

2 cups water

1 cup coconut cream

¼ cup toasted coconut (see sidebar)

½ cup finely chopped tropical fruits of your choice

1. Put the rice, water, and coconut cream in a medium-sized saucepan and mix well. Bring to a boil over medium-high heat. Reduce heat and cover with a tight-fitting lid. Cook for 15 to 20 minutes or until all of the liquid has been absorbed.

2. Let the rice rest off the heat for 5 minutes.

3. Fluff the rice and stir in the toasted coconut and fruit.

Mango Fool

A fool is usually a combination of heavy whipped cream and a fruit purée. The fruit is just barely folded into the cream, leaving slight stripes. This grown-up "pudding" is simple, light, and a true delight.

Serves 4-6

Ingredients

2 ripe mangoes, peeled and flesh cut from the pits

2 tablespoons lime juice

¼ cup sugar

1 cup heavy cream

1 tablespoon confectioners' sugar

Crystallized ginger (optional)

Mint leaves (optional)

1. Place the mangoes in a food processor with the lime juice and sugar. Purée until smooth.

2. In a large bowl beat the heavy cream with the confectioners' sugar until stiff.

3. Thoroughly fold the mango purée into the heavy cream.

85

4. Serve in goblets garnished with crystallized ginger or sprigs of mint, if desired.

Watermelon Ice

Chill your serving goblets for a frosty effect and to prevent the ice from melting once you shave it. Try different heirloom varieties of watermelon for an unexpected orange or yellow-colored ice!

Serves 6-8

Ingredients

⅓ cup water

½ cup sugar

1 (3-pound) piece of watermelon, rind cut away, seeded, and cut into small chunks (reserve a bit for garnish if desired)

1 tablespoon lime juice

Mint sprigs (optional)

1. Place the water and sugar in a small saucepan and bring to a boil. Remove from heat and allow to cool to room temperature, stirring frequently. Set the pan in a bowl of ice and continue to stir the syrup until cold.

2. Place the watermelon, syrup, and lime juice in a
   blender and purée until smooth.

3. Pour the purée through a sieve into a 9-inch baking
   pan. Cover the pan with foil.

4. Freeze the purée for 8 hours or until frozen.

5. To serve, scrape the frozen purée with the tines of a
   fork. Spoon the scrapings into pretty glass goblets
   and garnish with a small piece of watermelon or mint
   sprigs.

Easy Thai Iced Tea

Thai iced tea in half the time — what's not to like? Add a shot of milk or condensed milk to make it extra creamy and delicious.

Yields 1 cup

Ingredients

2 tablespoons sugar

1–2 tablespoons Thai tea leaves

1 cup hot water

Ice

1. Put the sugar into a large glass.

2. Place the tea leaves in a tea ball and place it in the glass.

3. Add the hot water. Let steep until done to your preferred strength.

4. Stir to dissolve the sugar and add ice.

Asian Carrot Sticks

No five-spice? No problem! You can make your own by combining Szechuan peppercorns and star anise (toasted and put through a spice grinder), with ground cloves, ground cinnamon, and ground fennel seeds.

Serves 4-6

Ingredients

1 pound thin carrots, peeled and cut into quarters lengthwise

4 tablespoons water

4 tablespoons olive oil

2 cloves garlic, minced

2 tablespoons rice vinegar

⅛–¼ teaspoon cayenne pepper

½–1½ teaspoons paprika

½–1 teaspoon Chinese five-spice powder

3 tablespoons cilantro, chopped

Salt and pepper to taste

1. Place the carrots in a pan large enough to hold them comfortably. Cover the carrots with water and bring to a boil over high heat. Drain the carrots and return them to the pan.

2. Add the 4 tablespoons of water, the olive oil, and the garlic; bring to a boil, reduce to a simmer, and cook until just tender. Drain.

3. In a small bowl, stir together remaining ingredients; pour over the carrots, tossing to coat.

4. Season to taste with salt and pepper.

5. The carrots may be eaten immediately, but develop a richer flavor if allowed to marinate for a few hours.

Thai-Style Guacamole

Take a traditional Mexican dip, add ginger, and it gets an Asian makeover. Serve alongside fried wontons to complete the Far East theme.

Yields 2 cups

Ingredients

2 ripe avocados, pitted and chopped

4 teaspoons lime juice

1 large plum tomato, seeded and chopped

1 tablespoon onion, chopped

1 small garlic clove, minced

1 teaspoon grated lime zest

1 teaspoon grated gingerroot

1 teaspoon serrano or jalapeño chili, chopped

1–2 tablespoons cilantro, chopped

Salt and freshly ground black pepper to taste

1. Place the avocado in a medium-sized bowl. Add the lemon juice and coarsely mash.

2. Add the remaining ingredients and gently mix
   together.

3. Serve within 2 hours.

Thai Chicken Salad

Chinese (or Napa) cabbage has more delicate leaves and mouth-feel than traditional red or green savoy cabbage. If needed you can substitute with the latter, but make sure you shred it finely and expect a heavier salad.

❧

Serves 4

Ingredients

For the dressing:

¼ cup vegetable oil

2 tablespoons rice wine vinegar

1 tablespoon soy sauce

2 teaspoons grated gingerroot

Pinch of sugar

¼ teaspoon (or to taste) salt

For the salad:

2 cups cooked chicken, chopped

4 ounces snow peas, trimmed

3 green onions, trimmed and sliced

1 cup bean sprouts

1 medium head of Chinese cabbage, shredded

1 tablespoon toasted sesame seeds

1. Place the salad dressing ingredients in a small bowl and whisk vigorously to combine.

2. In a medium-sized bowl, combine the chicken, snow peas, green onions, and bean sprouts. Add the dressing and toss to coat.

3. To serve, arrange the cabbage on a serving platter. Mound the chicken salad over the cabbage. Garnish with the sesame seeds.

Peanut Potato Salad

The pairing of peanuts and mint is a classic Thai combo that's used with great results here. Choose all-natural peanut butter for a more savory flavor; traditional brands for a hint of sweetness.

Serves 8-10

Ingredients

3 pounds boiling potatoes, peeled

1 cup salted peanuts, coarsely chopped, divided

1 medium-sized red bell pepper, cored and chopped

2 stalks celery, sliced

4 green onions, trimmed and sliced

¼ cup cilantro, chopped

¼ cup mint, chopped

¾ cup mayonnaise

¼ cup peanut butter

3 tablespoons rice vinegar

Salt and pepper to taste

1. Bring a large pot of water to a boil over high heat. Add the potatoes and cook until tender. Drain and cool. Cut into ½-inch cubes.

2. In a large bowl, combine the potato cubes, ¾ cup of peanuts, red bell pepper, celery, green onion, cilantro, and mint.

3. In a small bowl, whisk together the mayonnaise, peanut butter, and vinegar. Season to taste with salt and pepper.

4. Pour the dressing over the potato mixture and toss to coat. Refrigerate for at least 1 hour. Garnish with the remaining peanuts before serving.

Southeast Asian Burgers

Serve alongside Fried Okra and Ginger Rice to create a Thai version of a drive-through meal!

Serves 4

Ingredients

1 clove garlic, minced

3 tablespoons bread crumbs

1 pound ground beef or ground turkey

¼ cup cilantro, chopped

¼ cup basil, chopped

¼ cup mint, chopped

2 tablespoons lime juice

1 teaspoon sugar (optional)

3 shakes Tabasco

1. In a medium-sized mixing bowl, combine all the ingredients.

2. Using your hands, gently mix the ingredients together and form 4 patties. Season each patty with salt and pepper.

3. Grill the patties to your liking, about 5 minutes per side for medium.

Spice-Poached Chicken

Once you infuse your poultry with this much flavor, you'll never want to cook it any other way. Serve shredded with steamed vegetables and sticky rice to let the spices shine.

Serves 4-6

Ingredients

1 whole star anise

½ teaspoon whole black peppercorns

½ teaspoon whole cloves

1 (2-inch) cinnamon stick

1 cardamom pod

¼ teaspoon dried tangerine peel (dried orange peel can be substituted)

5 cups water

¼ cup light soy sauce

2 tablespoons sugar

4–6 boneless, skinless chicken breasts

1. Place the star anise, peppercorns, cloves, cinnamon
   stick, cardamom pod, tangerine peel, and water in a
   stew pot. Bring the mixture to a boil over high heat.
   Let boil until the poaching liquid is reduced to 4
   cups.

2. Stir in the soy sauce and the sugar. Return the liquid
   to a boil.

3. Add the chicken breasts and reduce to a simmer.
   Poach the breasts until done, about 20 minutes.

Five-Spiced Vegetables

Here the five flavors of Asia — salty, hot, sweet, sour, and bitter — are found in the sauce. Add a little more honey if you prefer a sweeter sauce and fewer red pepper flakes if you don't want as much heat.

Serves 4

Ingredients

½ cup orange juice

1 tablespoon cornstarch

½–¾ teaspoon Chinese five-spice powder

¼ teaspoon crushed red pepper flakes

2 tablespoons soy sauce

2 teaspoons honey

1 tablespoon vegetable oil

1 pound mushrooms, sliced

1 cup carrot slices

1 small onion, halved and thinly sliced

1–2 cloves garlic, minced

3 cups broccoli florets

1. In a small bowl, combine the orange juice, cornstarch, five-spice powder, red pepper flakes, soy sauce, and honey; set aside.

2. Heat the vegetable oil in a wok or skillet over medium-high heat. Add the mushrooms, carrots, onion, and garlic. Stir-fry for approximately 4 minutes.

3. Add the broccoli and continue cooking another 2 to 4 minutes.

4. Stir in the sauce. Cook until the vegetables are done to your liking and the sauce is thick, approximately 2 minutes.

5. Serve over rice noodles, pasta, or rice.

Peninsula Sweet Potatoes

Coconut milk infuses an island flavor to any dish, and this is no exception! If you want to mash the sweet potatoes once they are cooked, that's another great way to enjoy them.

Serves 4

Ingredients

1 pound sweet potatoes or yams of varying varieties, peeled and cut into bite-sized pieces

1 bay leaf

1 teaspoon sugar

¼ teaspoon salt

1 (14-ounce) can coconut milk

1. Place the sweet potato pieces in a large saucepan. Add just enough water to cover them, and bring to a boil. Add the bay leaf and cook until the potatoes are soft. Remove the bay leaf and discard.

2. Stir in the sugar and salt. After the sugar has dissolved, remove the pan from the heat and stir in the coconut milk. Adjust the seasonings by adding salt and/or sugar if necessary. Adjust the consistency by adding more water and/or coconut milk.

Honeyed Chicken

More satisfying — and healthier! — than the fried version, this sweet and sour chicken dish beats anything you could order from the takeout menu.

Serves 3-4

Ingredients

2 tablespoons honey

2 tablespoons fish sauce

2 tablespoons soy sauce

½ teaspoon Chinese five-spice powder

2 tablespoons vegetable oil

1 medium onion, peeled and cut into wedges

1 pound boneless, skinless chicken breasts, cut into bite-sized pieces

3–4 cloves garlic, thinly sliced

1 (1-inch) piece ginger, peeled and minced

1. Combine the honey, fish sauce, soy sauce, and five-spice powder in a small bowl; set aside.

2. Heat the oil in a wok on medium-high. Add the onion and cook until it just begins to brown.

3. Add the chicken; stir-fry for 3 to 4 minutes.

4. Add the garlic and ginger, and continue stir-frying for 30 more seconds.

5. Stir in the honey mixture and let cook for 3 to 4 minutes, until the chicken is glazed and done to your liking.

Fruit in Sherried Syrup

This is a simple, elegant dessert. The syrup keeps in the fridge for up to a week and can be made in advance for easy dinner-party prep. You can also use it as a simple syrup to flavor water or tea!

Serves 4-6

Ingredients

2 tablespoons sugar

4 tablespoons water

2 tablespoons dry sherry

2 teaspoons lemon juice

1 orange, peeled and segmented

2 cups fresh pineapple chunks

1½ cups kiwi slices

1. In a small saucepan over high heat, boil the sugar and the water until syrupy. Remove from the heat and let cool to room temperature. Stir in the lemon juice and sherry; set aside.

2. In a serving bowl, combine the orange segments, the pineapple chunks, and the kiwi. Pour the syrup over the fruit and toss to combine. Refrigerate for at least 1 hour before serving.